THE
Archive Photographs
SERIES

WISBECH

A rare picture of Lilian Ream at work.

THE
Archive Photographs
SERIES

WISBECH

Compiled by
Kim Bowden and David Rayner
from the Lilian Ream Collection

CHALFORD

First published 1996
Copyright © Kim Bowden, David Rayner
and Lilian Ream Exhibition Gallery, 1996

The Chalford Publishing Company
St Mary's Mill, Chalford,
Stroud, Gloucestershire, GL6 8NX

ISBN 0 7524 0740 6

Typesetting and origination by
The Chalford Publishing Company
Printed in Great Britain by
Redwood Books, Trowbridge

Contents

Introduction

Wisbech is a small east coast port and market town, which grew, particularly in the eighteenth and nineteenth centuries, to serve the rich agricultural land which surrounds it. Situated on the banks of the river Nene, a few miles inland from the shallow waters of the Wash, Wisbech has been a port of call for east coast trading vessels and those from the Baltic and Russia since the early Middle Ages.

The Fens which surround Wisbech were largely drained in the seventeen and eighteenth centuries when the marshes and meres so beloved by the local fishermen and wildfowlers were turned into the richest agricultural land in the country. The town became a centre for small businesses which served the needs of local farmers and industries which provided them with the equipment they needed. Regional auctions in the town sold their produce which was processed in local factories before it was transported to the rest of the country. The shops and markets provided for the local people who travelled in from the surrounding villages.

The photographs in this book all date from the first sixty odd years of the twentieth century and all form part of the Lilian Ream Exhibition Gallery collection. This period saw great changes in the way people lived across the whole world and even in a relatively small town the pace of technological and social change still had a major impact. Some of these great changes are illustrated in this book.

Lilian Ream was a remarkable woman who ran a number of businesses in Wisbech including the Borough Studio. She started her photographic career, at the age of 17, as an apprentice to Alfred Drysdale, a Wisbech photographer and after working with a number of other local firms she started her own studio in 1909. In time she took over the other photographic businesses in Wisbech and became a well-known figure in the area until her retirement, at the age of 72, in 1949. The family firm she built continued until 1971 and over this period amassed a large collection of photographic negatives.

The negatives from which these photographs have been printed were all taken either by Lilian Ream herself or by members of her staff. The Lilian Ream Studio recorded local people, places and events. It was very much a commercial operation and the variety of scenes reflect the variety of customers which ranged from both local newspapers, to shops, factories, sports teams and individuals who wanted to record their family, home or some major happening in their lives. Portraits were the 'bread and butter' of the business and form about seventy per cent of the collection. They illustrate not only changeing fashions in clothes but also the way people saw themselves, their families and their place in the world.

No one knows just how many negatives existed when the firm closed down as all the records have since disappeared but many were lost before the surviving negatives, numbering approximately 100,000 were acquired by Cambridgeshire Libraries in 1981. They were sorted with the aid of an MSC project sponsored by Fenland District Council and later a number of successful exhibitions were held thanks to sponsorship by local businesses. Unfortunately many of the negatives are in very poor condition and are deteriorating all the time. Cambridgeshire County Council were unable to provide the funds needed to save the collection and in 1993 handed them over to a newly formed charitable trust in the hope that it would be better able to raise the finance required. The trust has continued trying to make more of the collection available to the public but progress on conservation is extremely slow.

Some of the images in this book illustrate the problems of damage and chemical disintegration and show how without urgent work many of the images will be lost in the future. As mentioned earlier most of the records relating to the negatives were destroyed. The only remaining information which exists for most of the negatives is a serial number and the surname of the person who ordered the original photograph. Much of the information used in the captions has been collected from local people when the photographs have been displayed. We are grateful to all those who have searched their memories to help bring the pictures to life.

Sometimes memory can be inaccurate and we cannot always be sure that the information collected is correct. Nevertheless we hope the reader will gain some insights into the rapidly evolving world of the people who lived and worked in Wisbech in the last years before computers, supermarkets, the growth of television, the mass ownership of cars and all the other technological advances increased the pace of change to such a degree that even events of forty years ago seem to belong to a different age.

One
Town Scenes

Wisbech port, 1912. Looking downstream, on the left is North End with the light railway which ran from the Old Market, through the port and linked up with the Midland and Great Northern railway line. In the centre, a ship bringing timber from the Baltic is being unloaded. On the right can be seen Mills Brewery, in front of which, largely obscured by the buildings in the foreground, are the railings marking the side of the canal. The canal entered the river through a lock below a road bridge.

Wisbech Market Place, 1928. The rides and side shows of the Mart were scattered around several sites in the town (see pp. 13, 104, 105) and here compete for space with the traditional Saturday market.

Parade to mark 'Shopping Week' in the Market Place, 1927. Shopping weeks were organised by the Wisbech Chamber of Trade to highlight the range of goods and services available in the town.

Motor Show in the Market Place, 1931. The Mermaid Inn, in the background, was demolished to make way for the HorseFair shopping precinct, which opened in 1988.

Display of army vehicles in Wisbech Market Place, during or just after the Second World War.

Opening of Woolworths store in the Market Place, 1928. The store still occupies the same site despite the many changes to the area.

Opening of Tesco supermarket in Wisbech Market Place in the 1960s. The publicity surrounding the opening of the first supermarket in the town attracted large crowds who were entertained by a procession.

The Iron Bridge across the River Nene in Wisbech, from the entrance to the Old Market, 1928. The Mart spread from the Market Place, down both sides of the river and into the Old Market (see p. 14, 15). The Iron Bridge was originally designed as a swing bridge which could open to allow shipping to pass up the river to Peterborough. However it was far too heavy for the mechanism which powered it and was soon fixed in place.

The Town Bridge and Clarkson Memorial, 1951. The new Town Bridge replaced the Iron Bridge in 1931. The tall memorial, designed by Sir Gilbert Scott, was erected in 1881 in memory of Thomas Clarkson, one of the leading campaigners for the abolition of slavery.

The east side of the Old Market, 1930s. Note the rails for the light railway which ran from the Old Market through the port.

Octagon church, Old Market, c. 1929. The octagon church was opened in 1831 in order to ease the overcrowding at the parish church of SS Peter and Paul. Originally there was a lantern tower similar to that at Ely Cathedral but this had to be removed as it was too heavy for the foundations.

North Street looking towards the Old Market, 10 December 1957.

The west side of the Old Market, early 1960s.

Chapel Road, looking towards the Old Market, c. 1910. Calves being herded for Overland and Ward, the livestock dealers, towards the cattle market.

The cattle market and The Chase, situated off Chapel Road, 1946. The bustling livestock markets no longer take place but the area is now the site of produce and antique auctions.

North Brink, Wisbech, in 1947. The Georgian houses of North Brink, with Peckover House in the centre, have lead to its description as one of the finest streets in the country. The winter of 1947/48 was exceptionally cold and ice flows can be seen floating on the river.

South Brink before the First World War. The Iron Bridge and the Clarkson Memorial can clearly be seen. The house on the right of the photograph was the birthplace of Octavia Hill, one of the founders of the National Trust and is now occupied by the Octavia Hill Museum. This negative has been badly affected by mould due to damp storage conditions.

Nene Quay, 1930. Looking downstream towards Mills Brewery and the gas holder. Horace Friend's warehouse has now been converted into flats but the lettering on the side has been retained. Leach and Son, printers, still operate from the same building although the lending library is no longer in existence.

Riverside warehouses backing on to the Old Market, 1969. With the decline in river trade and the building of the Freedom Bridge, these warehouses fell into disuse. Despite campaigns to save them for convertion into housing or a leisure complex, most were demolished in the 1980s.

Wisbech Canal, 1951. When the canal fell into disuse it rapidly deteriorated. Much of the poorer housing which lined this part of its route was also in a very bad condition.

The site of the Wisbech to Outwell Canal, 1965. After the canal was filled in, most of the streets of small terraced houses were demolished for redevelopment. Later, Churchill Road was built on much of the canal's course.

Ashworth's Yard, 1933. This area, off West Street, was redeveloped shortly after the photograph was taken.

Blackfriars Road, 1927. The large building was originally a residence known as Hill House, in Upper Hill Street, although only in the fens would this slight rise be termed a hill. Hill House was converted into an indoor market called Racey's Arcade, which is in the process of being demolished in this scene. The site is now occupied by the Empire Theatre.

West Street, c. 1930. Many of the town's narrow streets were not suitable for larger vehicles. It was served by a number of small bus operators and the rivalry between the firms could sometimes cause problems.

Alexandra Road, 1956. The road is pictured after a particularly heavy snowfall.

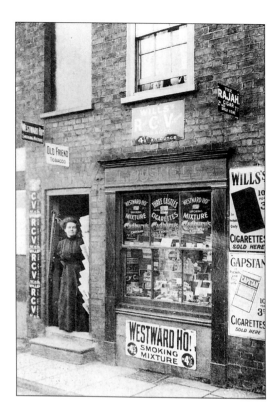

Mrs Bushell's shop, 2 Blackfriars Road, c. 1913.

The opening of the new Co-operative store, 1960s.

Fire drill at F Ford's store, 1929. This negative has badly cracked and peeling emulsion, which causes the black lines on the photograph, will, unless restored, eventually fall off and the image will be lost.

Henson's cycle shop, 1960s.

Hospital Sunday parade, 1937. Hospital Sunday was a day of celebration organised in order to raise funds for the local hospitals.

Hospital Sunday fund raisers, 1931.

Two

School Days

St Augustine's Infants School, 1914. The school was situated opposite St Augustine's church. The building is now known as Robert Hall Centre and is used by the local scouts.

Boys at St Peter's School display their certificates and medals, 1913. The school, which was situated in Stermyn Street, was demolished in the early 1960's.

Fancy dress group from St Peter's Boys School, 1930. In the background is the Falcon Warehouse, now occupied by Robert Hale, estate agents.

Girls from Wisbech High School set off on a school trip from Wisbech North station, 1932.

Boys from St Peter's School congregate at Wisbech East station prior to a school trip, 1955. The man at the back of the photograph, wearing a trilby hat, is 'Pop' Latham, who taught at the school for over forty years.

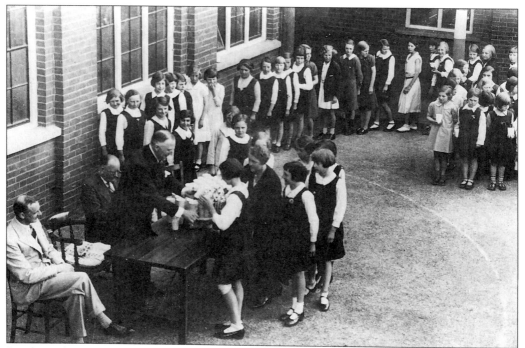

Pupils at the Queen's Girls School being presented with a commemorative mug to celebrate Empire Day, 1934.

Art class at the Queen's Girls School, 1934.

Carpentry lesson at the Grammar School, 1932.

First aid class at the Queen's Girls School, 1930s.

Victoria Road School football champions, 1926-27.

Sports day at Peckover School, 1955.

Children from St Audrey's Convent School, in Alexandra Road, play in the snow, 1930s.

Children enjoy the snow in Wisbech Park, 1933. The children include: Alfie and Freddie Clark, Dick Elsey, Ray Hyam, Don Nicholls, ? Bouch, Billy Merry, Dorothy Nicholls, Jack Merry, Claude Overland, Betty Hyam, Hazel Nicholls, M. Rouse, Eileen Swain and Neville Hyam.

Christmas party at St Mary's Catholic Infants School, 1963.

Children demonstrate new equipment at the opening of the Peckover School, in Leverington Road, 1953.

Three
People at Work

Most of the local industry in Wisbech revolves around agriculture and its products.

Queueing for work in 1933. A party of girls who have travelled from Scotland wait outside Wisbech employment office in the hope of obtaining work.

Produce auctions at Cross's Auction Hall, Chase Street in 1946 (top) and 1950 (bottom).

Outdoor strawberry auction on the Old Market, 1953. The site of these regular Saturday sales of local produce was known as the 'Stones'.

Pre-Christmas poultry sale, 1962.

Sale of vehicles belonging to Frank Williams Ltd, 1957.

Wisbech market, 1934.

The canning industry has been a major employer in Wisbech for many years. Grading peas, c. 1965.

Smedley's canning factory in 1931. The canned vegetables are stacked in large metal baskets ready for cooking.

Chip baskets, or punnets, were made in vast quantities at several Wisbech factories for the fruit picking industry. Wood arrives at J. W. Burton's factory, c. 1910.

Chip baskets being made at English Brothers, 1950's.

Chip baskets being made at the British Basket Company, 1960.

The vast quantities of chip baskets produced can be seen in English Brothers' warehouses, 1950.

The bottling line at Elgood's Brewery, on North Brink, supervised by Joan Stallon and her brother, Les, in 1951.

Hops being added to the brewing process, 1965. Elgood's Brewery has been established in the town for over 200 years.

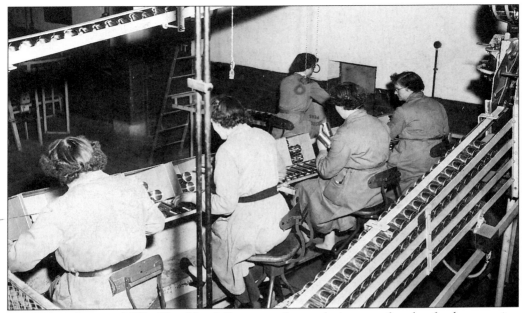

Metal Box factory, 1956. The Metal Box manufactured tin cans for the food processing industry.

Burall's printing works, 1962. The town has a reputation for fine printing. Burall's is one of a number of local family firms which started in the nineteenth century and continue today.

Wisbech post office sorting room, 1931.

A local family bakery, 1960s.

Fred Boston's building firm, from Murrow, near Wisbech, making repairs to a church. The firm is still in operation, but this a copy of an earlier photograph.

W.G. West's, local builders, at work in 1951.

Nene Quay, 1929. The river bank was piled and a new roadway built prior to the construction of the new Town Bridge, (see p. 73).

Reinforcing the riverbed with stone, 1932. This work needed to be done regularly in order to stop the fast-flowing current scouring the bed and undercutting the foundations of the Town Bridge, which is built on a bend in the river.

Building of new sluice, 1930. With the decline of water transport, the canal ceased to function commercially and the lock, which allowed access to the River Nene for barge traffic, was replaced by a sluice.

Loading from a warehouse on the west bank of the river, 1930. The River Nene has a considerable tidal range enabling a sloping conveyor belt to be used at low tide.

Loading potatoes, 1927. In the early days much of the loading of ships was done by men carrying individual sacks straight off the backs of delivery lorries. Note the tracks of the light railway which served the docks.

Unloading timber, 1933. The importation of Scandinavian and Russian timber has been important to Wisbech for many years. It was unloaded by hand and carried up sloping planks which rested on trestles, over the road, to be stacked in the adjoining timber yards.

A similar scene in 1951. Cranes and trucks have replaced much of the manual labour.

Watt's blacksmiths shop, 1929. This shop was situated in the Horsefair. The owner is working in the centre with Jack Earish to his right.

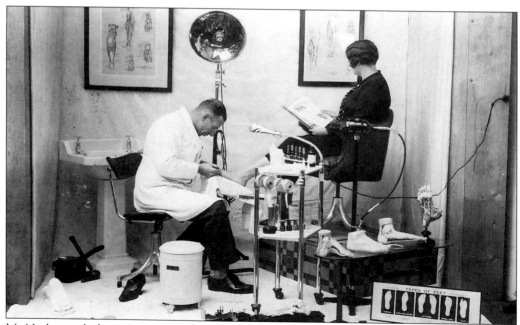

Mr Narborough demonstrates the latest in chiropody at a trades fair held in Wisbech, 1933.

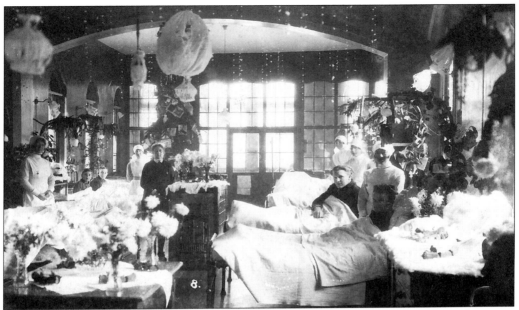

Christmas celebrations in the North Cambs Hospital in 1929 (top) and 1958 (bottom).

Group portrait of the staff of Keiller's preserves factory, 1921.

Staff of the Woolworth's store pictured on the roof in 1967.

Four
Agriculture

Horse drawn reaper/binder at work, c. 1925. The reaper/binder cut and tied the corn into bundles which were stacked, on end, in stooks to dry before threshing.

Harvesting at Brigstock's Farm, near Wisbech in 1929.

Horse drawn wagon before the First World War.

Harvesting at Sir Walter West's farm at Upwell in 1930. The corn stooks are loaded onto single horse carts to be taken from the fields to the farmyard where it is threshed, using a steam driven threshing machine, and the straw stacked.

Mrs Harrod, of Barroway Drove, 1953.

Cattle Show, 1928.

Plucking geese for the Christmas market, c. 1910. This is a copy of an early photograph made by the studio as one of the services it offered. The original photograph had been folded making a vertical crease mark on the left hand side.

Norfolk Bronze turkeys and their proud owner, 1932.

Interior of an ancient barn near Wisbech, c. 1935.

Loading apples into railway trucks, 1960.

Children of the Holland family, feeding the chickens, 1916.

Potato picking gang on Hickman's Farm, 1934.

Strawberry pickers on Image's Farm, 1931. The pickers have spare baskets, locally called 'chips', attached to their waists (see pp. 38 & 39).

Flower picking, 1930. Whole families travelled to the fens every year for the harvest. They were contracted to live and work on particular farms. While the adults worked, students from Cambridge University would look after their children.

London fruit pickers and their families arrive at Wisbech East station in 1936. The families would be collected from the station by the farmers they were contracted to and taken out to the farms where they would live and work throughout the summer.

Students advertising a dance at the Corn Exchange in 1926. As well as looking after the children the students also organised some entertainment for their parents.

Mother and children on Ayre's Farm in 1929.

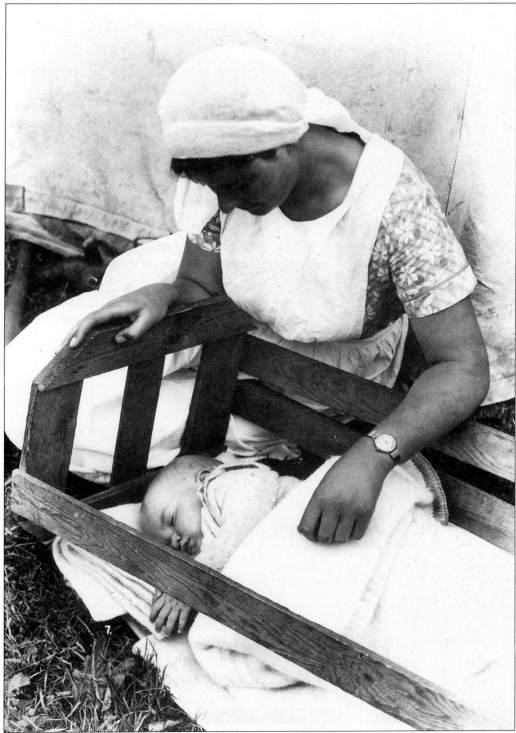

Student caring for a baby on Hickman's farm on 28 June, 1933.

Entertaining the children at Fitton End, Gorefield, in 1939.

Students and children, 1929. The wealthier students often brought their own cars to the camps and these always proved a popular attraction.

Five

Events

The demolition of the octagon church, 1952. The Trustees Savings Bank now stands on the site vacated by the church. Note the sign 'pews for sale' to the right of the entrance.

Firemen fight a fire at the Corner House cafe, 28 June 1952. The Corner House Cafe was situated at the corner of the Market Place, above the Scotch Wool and Hosiery Stores, which are now the premises of the British Heart Foundation shop.

Damping down after a fire on an industrial site in Wisbech, 1929.

The aftermath of a fire at Crabtree's Garage, Church Terrace, *c.* 1925. The garage was situated opposite St Peter's church on what is now the site of Westgate House, china and glass department.

Aerial view of the fire at Crabtree's Garage taken from the tower of St Peter's church.

The *Hansa*, 8 September - 5 October 1935. The *Hansa*, with 1600 tonnes of timber on board, was travelling from Russia when it ran into severe storms. The timber on deck became waterlogged and had to be jettisoned to stop the ship from keeling over. The ship ran aground whilst moving up the River Nene towards Wisbech and more of the cargo had to be disposed of in order to float her off. As both the bottom plating and the engines had been damaged in the grounding, tugs had to be sent from Hull to tow her in. The port was closed to traffic for over a week by all the loose timber floating in the river.

SS Hasselburg, 20 August 1933. After discharging a cargo of timber in Wisbech, the *Hasselburg* was being piloted downriver on her journey to the Tyne, when she ran aground near Foul Anchor. Note the tiny figures under the hull near the bow.

Barge accident near Elgood's Brewery, North Brink, 21 April 1931. The barges were carrying stone upriver when one struck the bank and sank dragging the others with it.

Tidal flooding in North Terrace, 1961. The Oak public house on the right of the picture stood at the top of Sandyland.

The dismantling of the railway bridge at Wisbech East station, 1961.

Workmen deal with a derailment, 1929.

This accident occurred at the Weasenham Lane crossing in 1932.

Recording the popular radio show, *Have a go*, 1957. Mrs Sheila Chesters, founder of the Little Theatre group, is pictured with the host, Wilfred Pickles. Mabel can be seen 'at the table'.

Celebrity concert by the Wisbech Male Voice Choir at the Empire Theatre, 1952. In the front row, second from the right, is Semprini and, holding the basket of flowers, the young Julie Andrews.

Pop star Adam Faith pays a visit to Wisbech, 1962.

'Ah yer got a loight bor?', 1968. The popular Singing Postman pictured at a local traction engine rally.

General Election campaign, 1951. Prime Minister, Clement Attlee, broadcasting from the Market Place.

Tory party leader, Ted Heath, visits a nursery at Walpole Cross Keys, 1965.

Construction and opening of the Wisbech Town Bridge, 1931. The bridge replaced the Iron Bridge, which was later dismantled, (see p. 44).

These four photographs show some of the Celebrations for the Silver Jubilee of King George V and Queen Mary, 1935.

The proclamation of Queen Elizabeth II is read outside the Corn Exchange, 1952. The Aldermen include J. Shawl, J. Ollard, A. Humphrey, A. Mellor, A. Hunter-Rowe and J. Penny.

This photograph, and the two opposite, show Coronation celebrations, 1953. The procession passes along Bridge Street.

Street party in Southwell Road.

Procession of floats on the river at Outwell.

Gathering in the Market Place to celebrate the Cambridgeshire Agricultural Show, 1932. The show was opened by Prince George, Duke of Kent, who can be seen in the centre of the platform.

Queen Mary in Museum Square, 1951. The Queen was paying a visit to the Wisbech and Fenland Museum.

Six

War

Three Wisbech soldiers in First World War uniforms.

The Smith family in 1916. Many servicemen visited the studio for photographs of themselves and their families.

The funeral of Trooper Cockett in 1916.

Armistic Day service at Wisbech War Memorial, 1929.

Members of the British Legion leave for a tour of the Western Front battlefields, 1932.

Territorials leaving Wisbech on exercise between the wars (above and below).

Digging trenches for air raid shelters in Hazel Gardens, 1938.

Recruitment campaign for the Air Raid Patrol, 1942.

Member of the ATS, 1943.

Troops leaving Wisbech East station, 1939.

Members of the WRVS demonstrate an emergency soup kitchen, 1945.

Evacuees party. Many children from inner cities were evacuated to live in the area during the war.

Victory parade through Wisbech in 1945. A local youngster with his mascot (top) and women of the Land Army (bottom).

Civic celebrations to mark VE Day in Wisbech Park.

VE Day street parties. Dun Cow public house yard, at the top of Victoria Road (top) and Woodyard just off Norfolk Street (bottom).

Seven
Sport and Leisure

Skating on the frozen river at North End, c. 1910. Viewed from the bridge over the canal lock (see p. 9). Note the Harbour Line train on the far side of the river.

Ladies' river swim, 1929. Swimming races in the river were an annual event. The ladies swam from the Rifle Butts to the Town Bridge, a distance of approximately $1\frac{1}{2}$ miles.

Youngsters enjoying a swim at the old town swimming baths at Crab Marsh, 1933.

Scenes from a fishing match on the Middle Level Drain, 1927.

Cycling race, 1920s. Another very badly damaged negative.

Go-kart racing, 1962.

Music and movement in Wisbech Park, 1965.

Boys Brigade gymnastics display in the grounds of Wisbech Castle, 1926.

Boxing match, probably in the Corn Exchange, 1958.

Bowls match, 1931.

Wisbech football team, 1893.

Wisbech Town v Hastings, Fenland Park, 1968.

Croquet game at Bowthorpe Hall, 1913.

Post croquet match tea, at the Old Wisbech Grammar School, South Brink, 1932.

A lady tries her hand in the archery competition at a garden fete, 1928.

Stallholders and helpers at the Hospital Fete, 1928.

Scenes from Wisbech garden parties in 1912. The Honourable Alexandrina Peckover (top picture, seated second right, bottom picture, standing first right) and her sister, Hannah Jane (top picture, seated third right), were descendants of the famous Quaker banking family whose family home on North Brink is now a National Trust property.

A May Tea street party was held in Sandyland annually for the local children. Top: Alexandrina Peckover judges a fancy dress competition, 1934. Bottom: The tables laid out along the narrow street, 1933.

Wisbech Working Mens Club cribbage team, 1958.

Billiards competition, 1936.

A typical Victorian pub interior. This scene was taken in the Angel Hotel at the beginning of the century.

British Lion public house, 1966. The British Lion was situated at the corner of Ruby Street and Agenoria Street, near Blackfriars Bridge. Among the people in the photograph are landlord and lady Frank and Amy Sharpe, Harry Waterfield, Graham Crowson and John Waterfield.

A gathering of the Wisbech Standard Bunnies Club, 1931. The club was organised by the local newspaper and the picture shows the children at the Hippodrome Theatre, which was situated in Hill Street.

A scene from the play, *No No Nanette*, at the Empire Theatre, 1951.

Local dance band, The Amateur Co-optimists, 1930.

Local group, The Heppers, performing in 1958.

Opening of the Mart, 1953. A civic procession makes its way along the High Street before the Mayor officially opens the Mart. The Mart is a funfair which visits the town in March.

The civic party enjoy a ride on the Waltzers, 1953.

The Mart on the Old Market, 1930s.

The Mart on the Horsefair, 1951.

An elephant and its trainer parade in Bridge Street to advertise the forthcoming Robert Brothers circus, 1931.

The Bertram Mills circus big top is raised in the Horsefair, 1963.

A caged tiger, part of the Robert Brothers circus menagerie, 1933.

The band of Rosaire's circus on a visit to Wisbech in the 1930s.

Scenes from the Wisbech Rose Fair, 1960s.
The Rose Fair is an annual event held in the
summer to raise money for St Peter's church.

A Viking longship, one of the many floats in the Rose Fair procession, 1969.

Two girls enjoy a strawberry tea at the 1969 Rose Fair.

Four scenes from the 1929 Wisbech Pageant, 'Heart of the Fens'. Nearly 900 local people took part in this depiction of the history of Wisbech, which was written by Sir Arthur Bryant, the famous historian.

Scenes from the historical pageant held at Beaupre Hall, Outwell, in 1932.

Actors from the 1949 Wisbech Pageant.

Members of Hill Street holiday club making puppets, late 1960s.

Visitors to a trade exhibition in Wisbech Park display great interest in a model railway exhibit, 1957.

A party pose at Wisbech East station before an outing, c. 1908.

Day trip for staff from Smedley's canning factory, seen at Wisbech East station in 1949.

Football special pictured in 1958, prior to an away match at Bedford. The Poppies was the nickname of Wisbech Town Football Club.

Eight
People

The Lilian Ream Studio took tens of thousands of portraits of local people, both in the studio and at home. The following portraits offer a wonderful view of changing fashions and manners.

Mrs Bedmore and her daughter, Ann, 1913.

A studio portrait of a child to advertise a local charity collection.

Baby Cammack with seven puppies, 1945.

Miss Green in a studio portrait, taken in 1912. Miss Green is believed to have been one of Lilian Ream's earliest assistants.

First World War soldier and his wife. The soldier is seated on one of the many studio props.

The marriage between Mr Loughton and Miss Chapman took place in 1944.

The Strickland and Bailey families pose at a wedding in 1929.

The Bloodworth family on 17 December 1927.

The Thomas family pictured in 1913.

Mrs Piggot and her son, 1934. The Piggots are pictured in their new cottage, which has just been purchased with money from a legacy. Prior to this the poverty stricken pair had lived for several years in a small wooden shed.

Liberal supporters on the rear steps of Peckover House, 1929. From left to right: the Earl of Beauchamp, Graham Gardiner, Miss Alexandrina Peckover, Mrs de Rothschild, James de Rothschild MP and Charles Woodgate.

Members of the Scrimshaw family from
Murrow, near Wisbech, early 1900s.

A local character poses beside his letterbox which contains a nest of small birds.

Mrs and Mrs Thompson, 1939.

Acknowledgements

Thanks to all those who have supplied information about
photographs in the Lilian Ream Exhibition Gallery collection.

Photographic printing by:
Andrew Ingram
and
Anna Oakford

For further information about the collection please contact:
The Lilian Ream Exhibition Gallery
c/o Spindrift Print and Publishing
Second Marsh Road
Walsoken
Wisbech
PE14 7AB
Tel: (01495) 584855